TABLE OF CONTENTS

Here's what we'll cover ▽

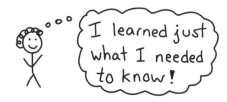

I learned just what I needed to know!

this code is undocumented, but I can handle that.

tricky bug? this will be fun! I'll fix it.

big underspecified problem? let's start!

How do I learn something that takes years to master?

wow! I learned SO MUCH at my job this year.

D0844061

How to be a Wizard Programmer

who can do <u>anything</u> (takes a very long time)

① ASK QUESTIONS. As long as there are people around you who know things you don't, ask them how to do things. Dumb questions. Scary-to-ask questions. Your questions will get less dumb <u>fast</u>.

② Run into a problem your coworkers don't know how to solve either.

③ DECIDE YOU WILL FIGURE OUT HOW TO SOLVE THE PROBLEM ANYWAY.
   (this is very hard but sometimes it works ☺)

The more programming I do, the more issues I run into where:

- I don't know
- my colleagues don't know
- Google doesn't know
- we gotta figure it out anyway

When this happens, I think:

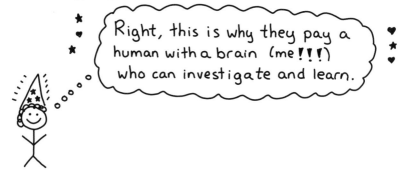

Right, this is why they pay a human with a brain (me!!!) who can investigate and learn.

This zine is about what the skill of "figure it out anyway" looks like.

When to invest in understanding?

We work with a lot of _abstractions_. You don't always need to spend time understanding how they all work under the hood.

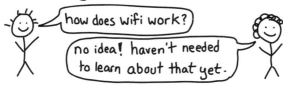

But a huge part of becoming a wizard is understanding how a seemingly magical computer system works.
When is it useful to spend time learning how a thing works?

① When you're trying to _debug_ a tricky problem
 → Sometimes the libraries you depend on have bugs.
 → Often, libraries/systems (like CSS or Linux) have complex abstractions (like the box model or epoll) that take time to learn.

② When you're trying to push the limits /optimize performance

For example, if you're writing data to a file you're always limited by the speed of your disks! Thinking about hardware can be important.

③ When you're trying to _innovate_

If you're building a new abstraction (like an async library), you gotta understand how the next layer down works! (epoll, select, etc.)

Asking good questions

One of my favorite tools for learning is asking questions of all the awesome people I know!

⋛ what's a good question? ⋛

good questions:

* are easy for the person to answer

* get you the information you're looking for

Here are some strategies for asking them:

state what you know

> so, I know when the database gets a lot of writes, the hard drive can't keep up.

> that's right! I don't think that was our problem, though. Look at this...

This helps because:

- I'm forced to think about what I know

- I'm less likely to get answers that are too basic or too advanced

Guessing the answer:

- makes me think!
- helps my coworker see what kind of answer I'm looking for

guess what the answer might be

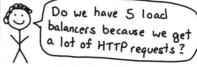

> Do we have 5 load balancers because we get a lot of HTTP requests?

> actually, we just want to be sure it's ok if one goes down.

choose who to ask

the database's creator

your coworker with a bit more experience than you

probably a better choice. Has a good shot at answering your question + way more time ☺

The person who knows the MOST isn't always the best person to ask!

Often, someone who learned more recently will remember better what it was like to not understand.

Especially if I have LOTS of questions, it's good to be respectful of their time ☺

find a good time

hey, can I ask you about database performance for 20 minutes?

yeah! after lunch!

ok!

do some research

so I found out that creating database indexes takes time, what happens if I run a query during index creation?

great

If I spend some time doing research first, I can ask a WAY BETTER question ☺

I ♥ asking yes/no questions like this because they're easier to answer and it means I have to focus the question carefully.

ask yes/no questions

does this database take out a lock when it does writes?

yes! Here are the docs you should read if you want to know more!

read the source code

Okay, but you can't ALWAYS ask people questions!

Sometimes:
- → there's no documentation
- → your coworkers are busy
- → or they don't know the answer
- → or you want to know A LOT more details than it is really reasonable to ask about

Luckily, we have open source!!!

I have an extremely specific question about the Linux kernel.

I would be DELIGHTED.

Linux kernel source

One day, I wanted to know if I could configure a socket on Linux to not queue connections. I googled and got some conflicting answers. But one of the Stack Overflow answers linked directly to the KERNEL CODE!

It looked basically like: hardcoded constant!

backlog = max(backlog, 8)

So it's impossible to set the backlog to 0.
It'll always end up being at least 8 ☺

tips for reading code

Here are some things I've found helpful when dealing with unfamiliar code:

When I see an error message I don't understand, searching the source for it is really easy and sometimes helps.

If the code I'm using is less than a few thousand lines, I like to quickly try to read it all to learn the basics of how it works.

Get your hands dirty!
- step through with a debugger!
- add tests!
- add print statements!
- introduce bugs!
- experiment!
- don't always trust the comments ☺

debugging: ♥ love your bugs ♥

(thanks to Allison Kaptur for teaching me this attitude!)
she has a great talk called "Love Your Bugs".

Debugging is a <u>great</u> way to learn. First, the harsh
reality of bugs in your code is a good way to reveal
problems with your mental model.

program — error: too many open files

I can't just open as many files as I want? Interesting!

Fixing bugs is also a good way to learn to write
more reliable code!

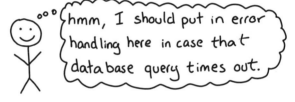

hmm, I should put in error handling here in case that database query times out.

Also, you get to solve a mystery and get immediate
<u>feedback</u> about whether you were right or not.

that's weird... ... oh goodness, that's a lot of errors ... I have an idea!

✓ coding a fix ... it works now! great work!

Nobody writes great code without writing + fixing lots of
bugs. So let's talk about debugging skills a bit!

how I got better at debugging

1 Remember: the bug is happening for a logical reason.

It's never magic. Really. Even when it makes no sense.

2 Be confident I can fix it

before: maybe this is too hard

now: Well I've fixed a lot of hard bugs before

3 Talk to my coworkers

? !

4 know my debugging toolkit

before:

I want to know $THING but I don't know how to find out

now:

I KNOW! I'll use tcpdump!

5 <u>most importantly</u>: I learned to like it

before:

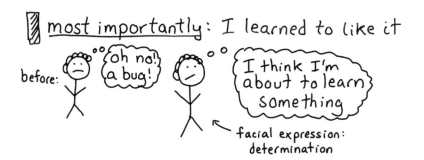

oh no! a bug!

I think I'm about to learn something

facial expression: determination

learning at work

Almost everything I spend time on day to day is something I've learned on the job.

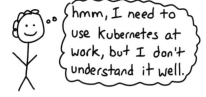

hmm, I need to use kubernetes at work, but I don't understand it well.

=>

set aside work time to:
- read source code
- ask questions
- watch talks
- read docs / blog posts
- do experiments

Debugging is one way to learn at work. Here are more ways!

follow up on bugs you couldn't figure out

ooh, someone else fixed that. Let's see how!

pay attention to others' code

this PR has some great ideas!

volunteer to do work that seems hard

I'm sure* I'll figure it out.

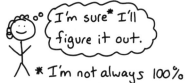

* I'm not always 100% sure, but it's worth trying!

watch more senior people operate

"that person does AWESOME work. How do they do it?"

don't: advocate for using something at work just because you want to learn it.

learning on my own

go to a conference

especially in an area
I don't know well
(like Linux kernel networking)

implement something that seems hard

gzip! tcp! keyboard driver!
debugger!

try a new tool

hmm, can I debug
Python with gdb?

pick a concept + spend 3 hours on it

b-trees! epoll! asyncio!

read a paper

Adrian Colyer's
"The Morning Paper"
has amazing paper
summaries

do some experiments

how many
requests/sec
can I serve
with Flask?

teach/blog it!

A huge part of my learning process is teaching as I learn!
Reasons it helps:

→ revisiting basic questions
  is important.

→ it forces me to realize
  when I don't actually
  understand something
  well yet.

How *does* asynchronous
programming work?

wait, I didn't realize
Unix groups did that!

learning to :design: software

It's surprisingly easy to end up in this situation:

A little bit of ♥ planning ♥ helps me make sure my hard work doesn't go to waste.

Here are a few things I find helpful to remember:

★ you can't predict how requirements will change

I just try my best and deal with changes when they come.

★ "good enough" is often really awesome

★ making a proof of concept can really help.

scenes from writing design docs

let's build expertise!

Let's zoom out a bit. A lot of the people I admire the most have been working on getting better at what they do for ⋆ years ⋆.

I've found it useful to pick a few things I'm really interested in (like Linux!) and focus on those.

Things I've spent significant amounts of time (at least a year) working on getting better at:

- Linux networking!
- debugging + profiling tools!
- machine learning!
- planning projects at work!
- technical writing / speaking!

There are lots of things (Go! Databases! Javascript!) that are important and I know a little about but haven't spent that much time on. That's okay!

It's super fun to see a progression like:

I'm going to learn about networking ... 6 months ... later ... wow, I'm a lot better at this now!

I think a) picking something to focus on and
b) *actively* working on getting better at it
is how all the people I admire got where they are

it's not too late to start learning

I started learning Linux in high school, in 2003. In 2013, after using it every day for 10 years, I realized something kind of scary:

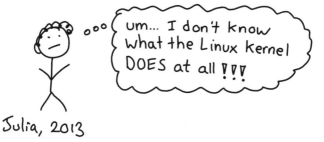

um... I don't know what the Linux kernel DOES at all ‼‼

Julia, 2013

There were all KINDS of concepts that I either didn't understand or didn't even know existed:

virtual memory   system call   ♡ futex ♡   interrupts
CPU scheduling   file descriptor   TCP

Just today (in 2017!), I realized I don't fully understand how Linux users/groups work. No big deal! I picked up my copy of "The Linux Programming Interface", read Chapter 9, and now I understand.

ugh, how can you not know that already?

today is the best day to start learning!

ways to build expertise